Fa la la la la la la la la

Level 1
Christmas Piano Favorites

Arranged by Mark Sarnecki

Fa la la la la la la la la © 2023 by Mark Sarnecki. All rights reserved.

All right reserved. No part of this book may be reproduced in any form or by electronic or mechanical means including Information storage and retrieval systems without permission in writing from the author.

ISNB: 1-896499-47-3

CONTENTS

Angels We Have Heard On High	6
Auld Lang Syne	24
Away In A Manger	10
The Coventry Carol	20
Deck The Halls	7
The First Noel	18
Good King Wenceslas	21
Hark The Herald Angels Sing	13
I Saw Three Ships	19
Jingle Bells	4
Jolly Old St. Nicholas	16
Joy To The World	17
O Christmas Tree	11
Silent Night	8
Up On The Housetop	12
We Three Kings	14
We Wish You A Merry Christmas	3
What Child is This?	22

We Wish You A Merry Christmas

Traditional

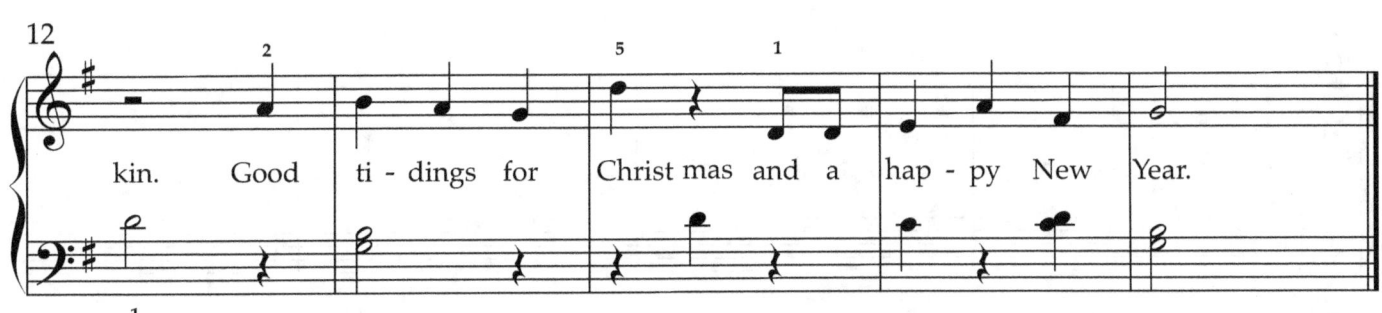

Jingle Bells

J. Pierpont

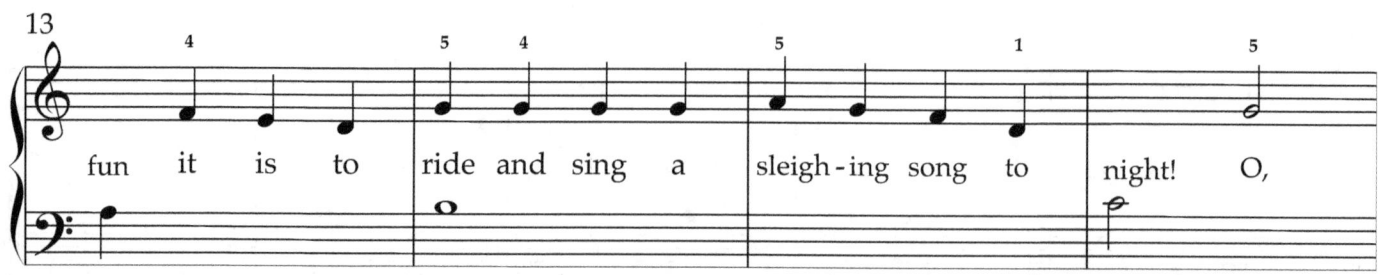

ANGELS WE HAVE HEARD ON HIGH

Traditional

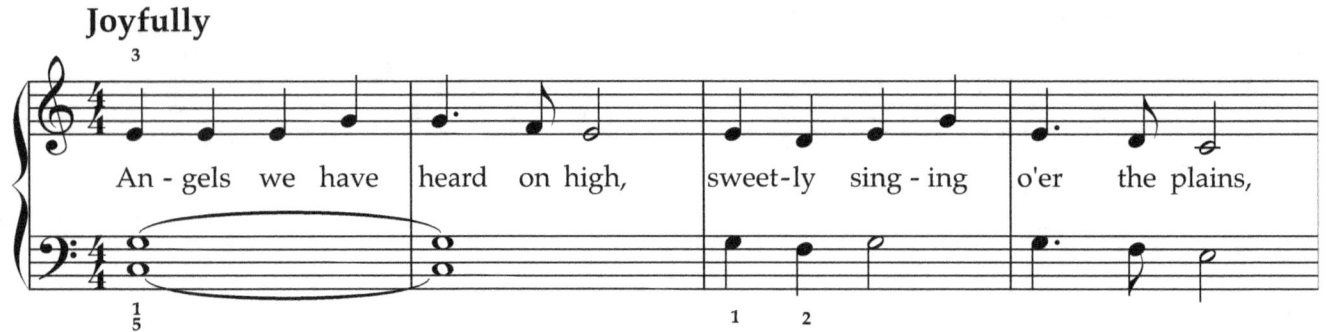
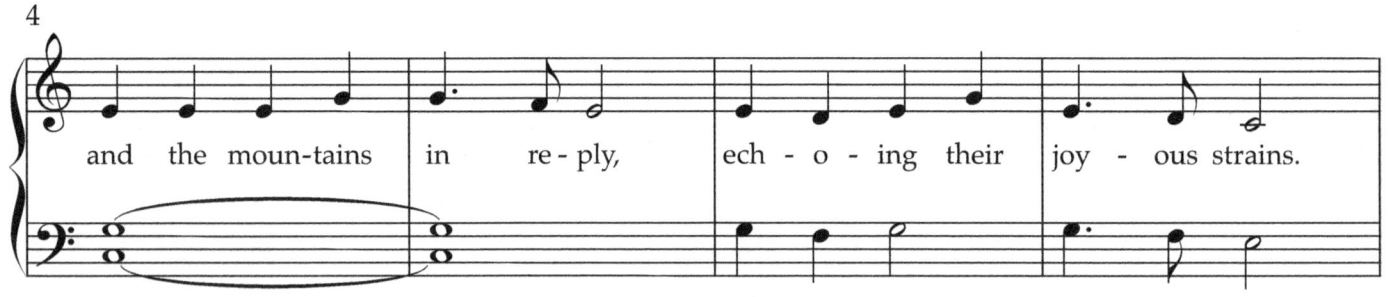
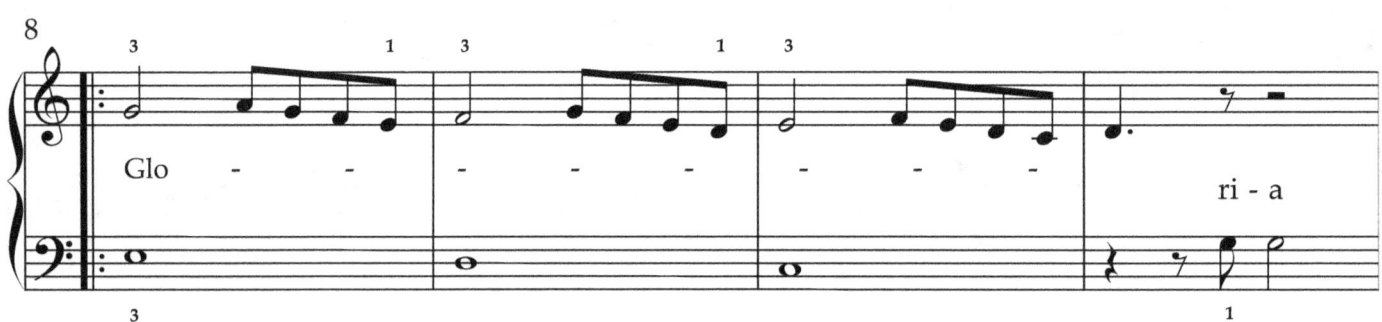
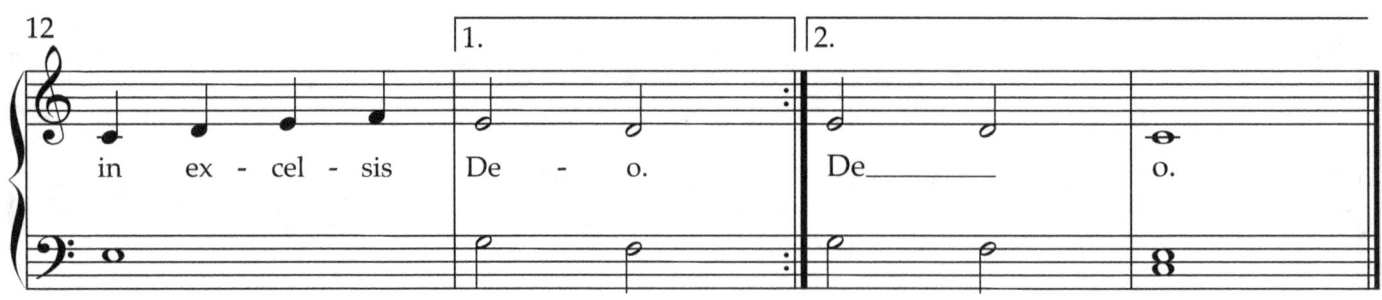

Deck the Halls

Traditional

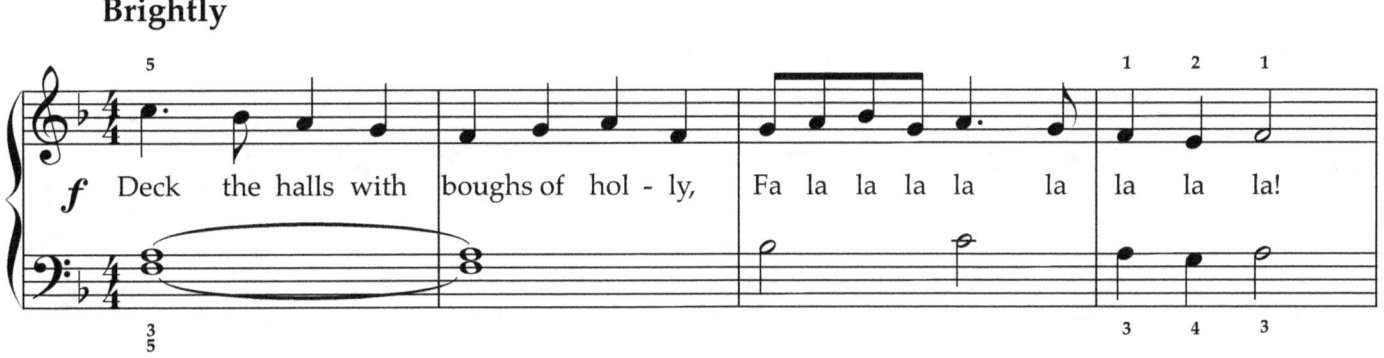

Silent Night

Franz Gruber

Gently

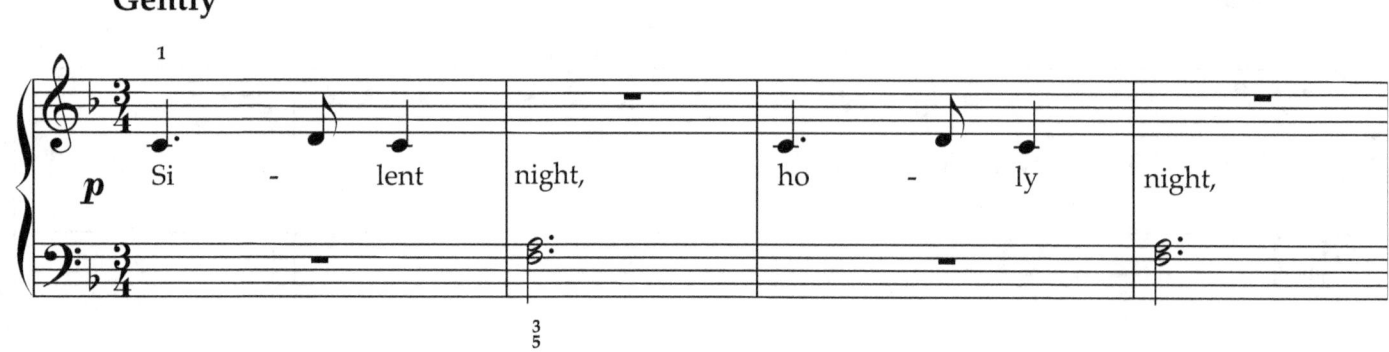
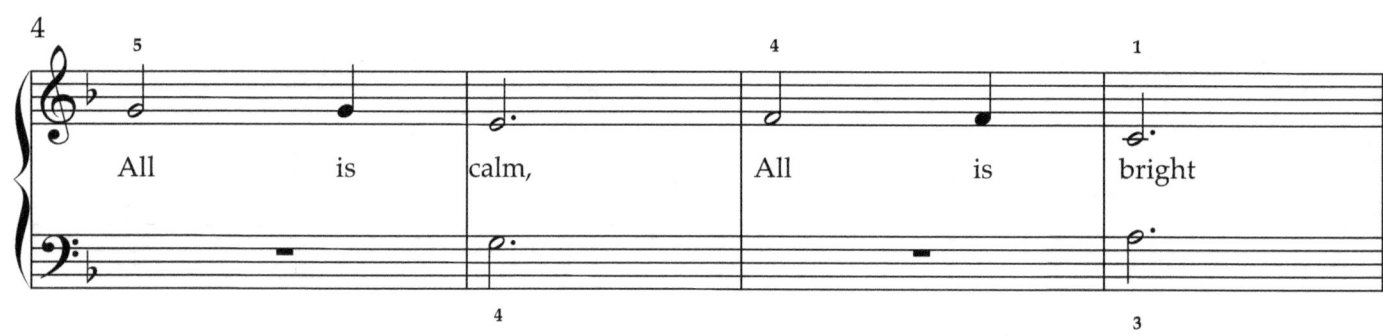
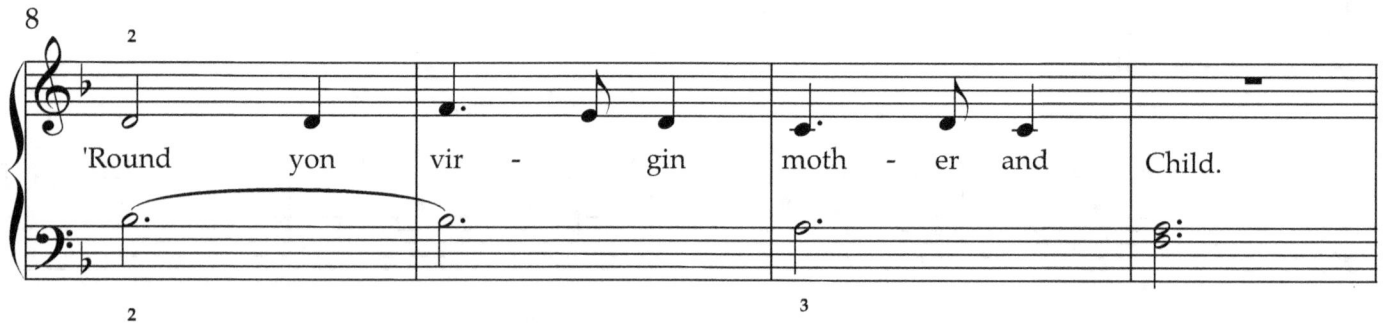

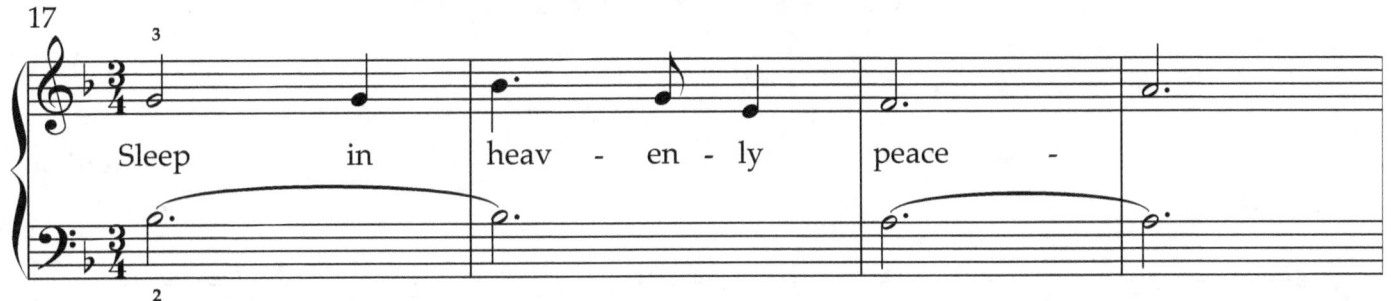
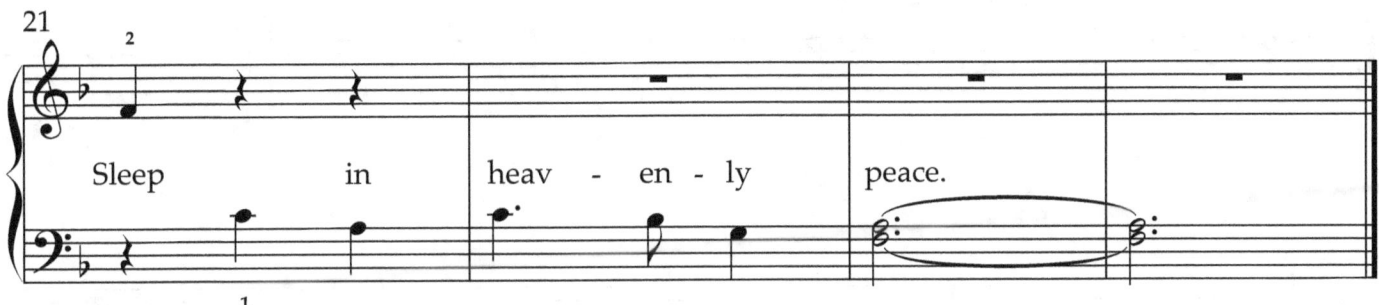

Merry Christmas!

Away in a Manger

Traditional

Tenderly

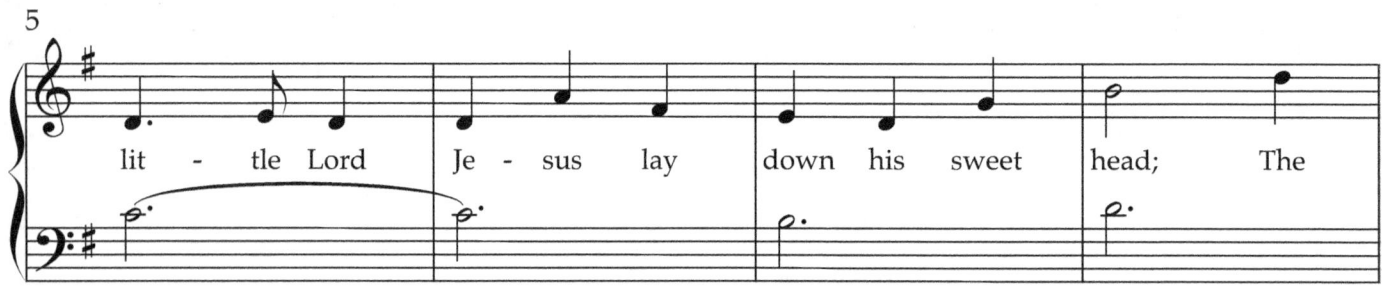

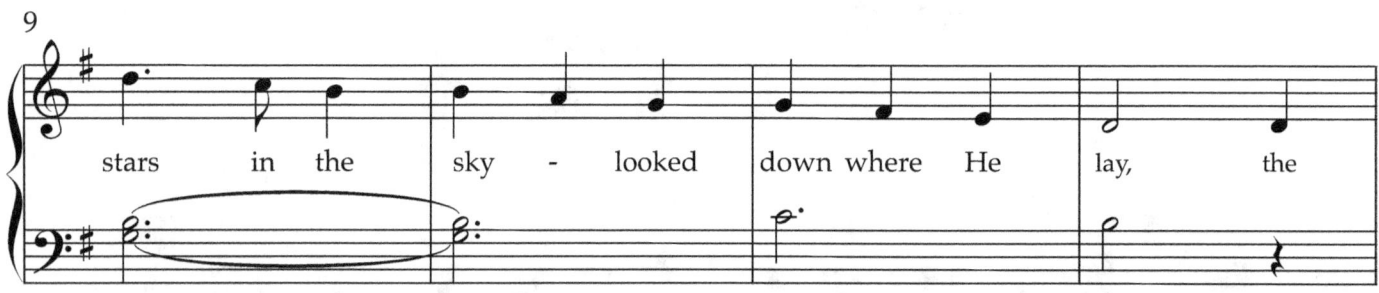

Oh Christmas Tree

Traditional

Moderately

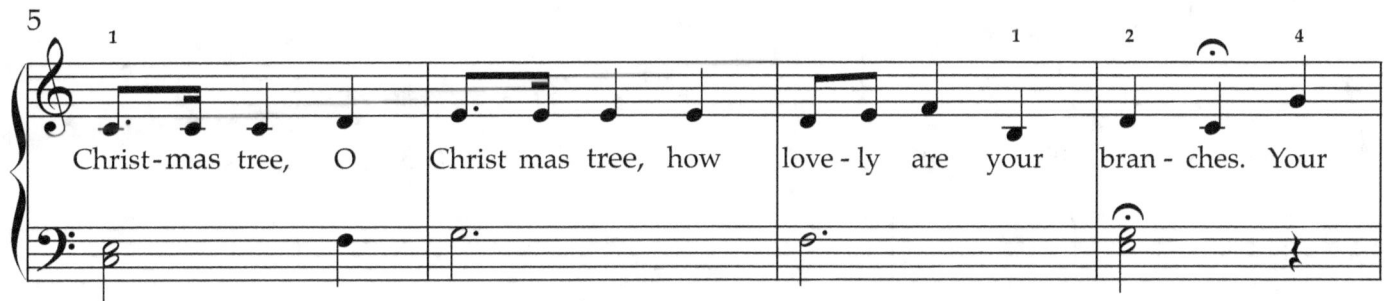

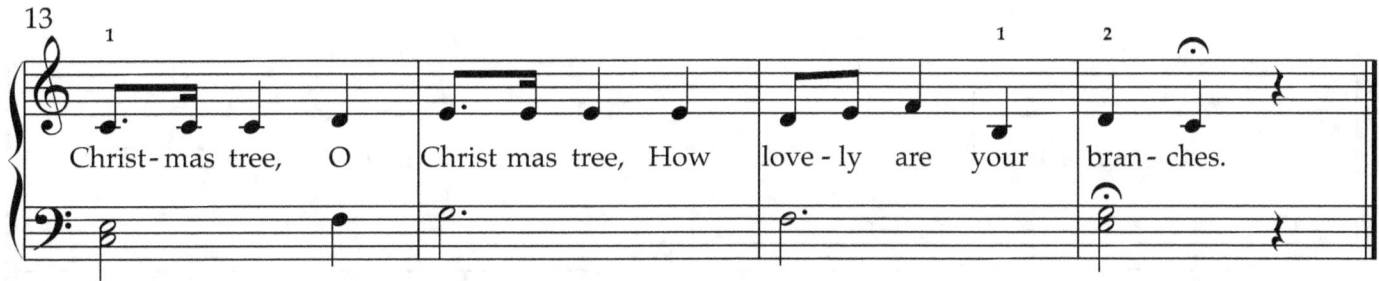

Up on the Housetop

Traditional

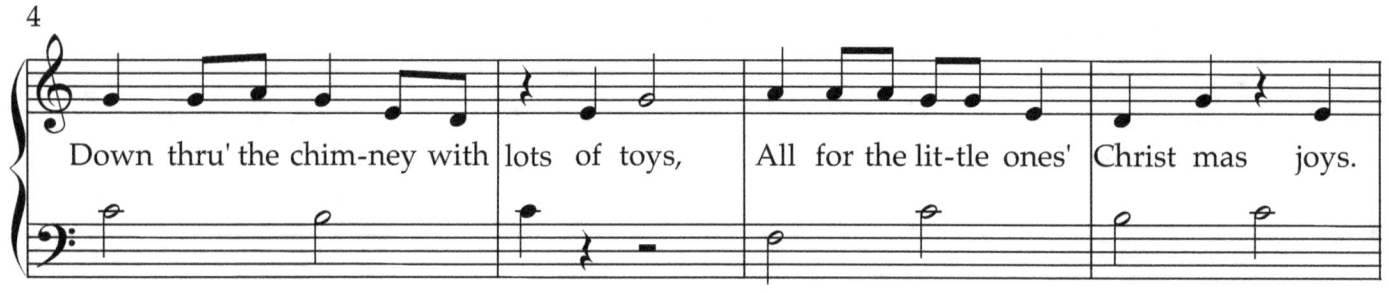

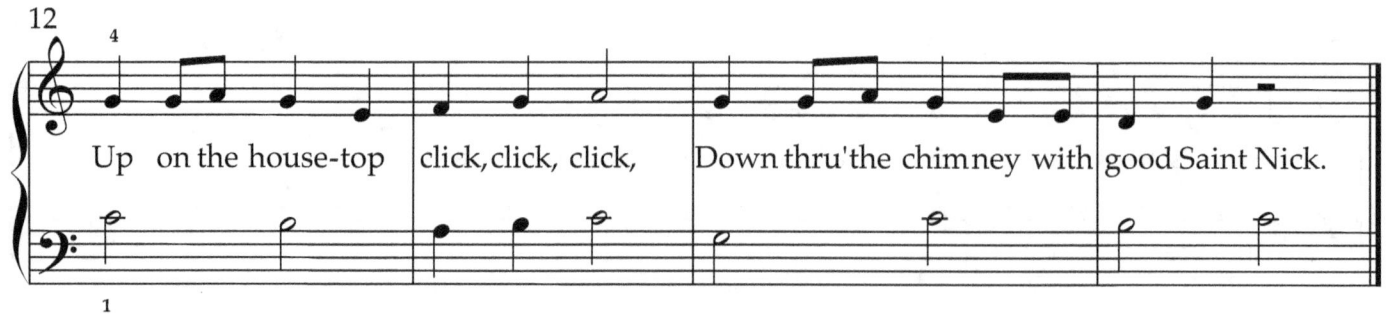

Hark the Herald Angels sing

Felix Mendelssohn

We three Kings

John Henry Hopkins

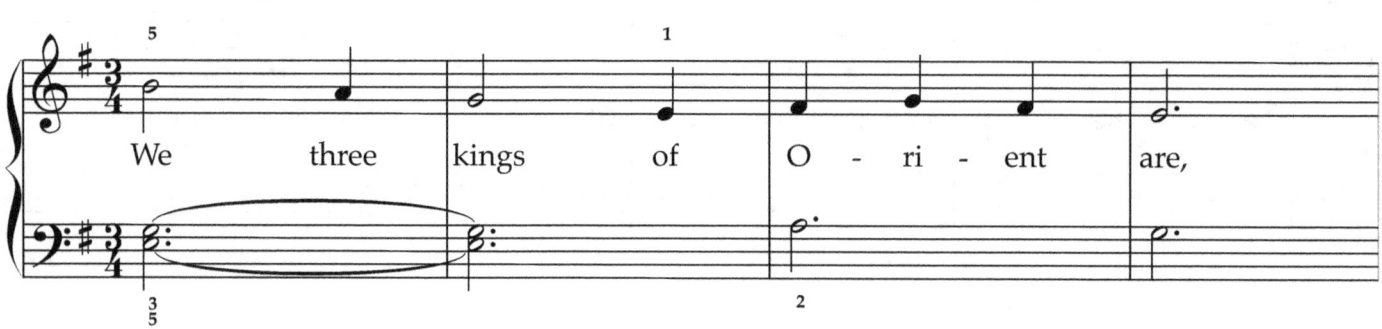

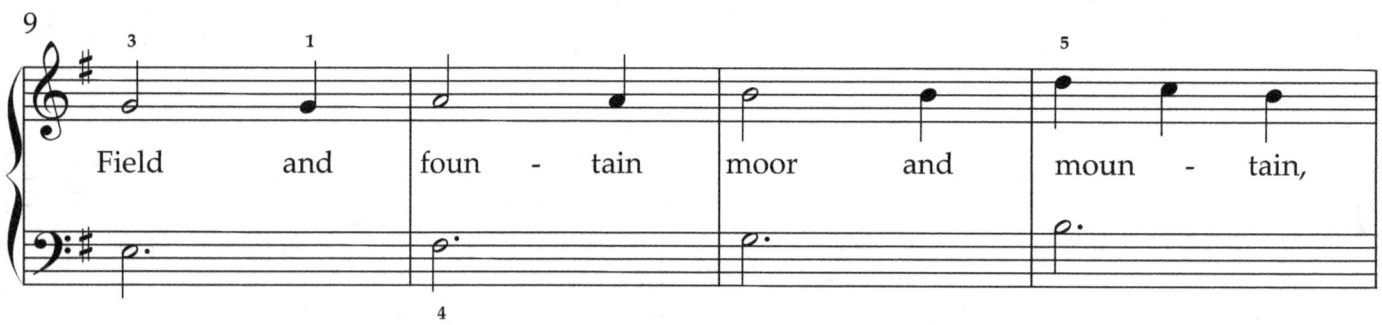

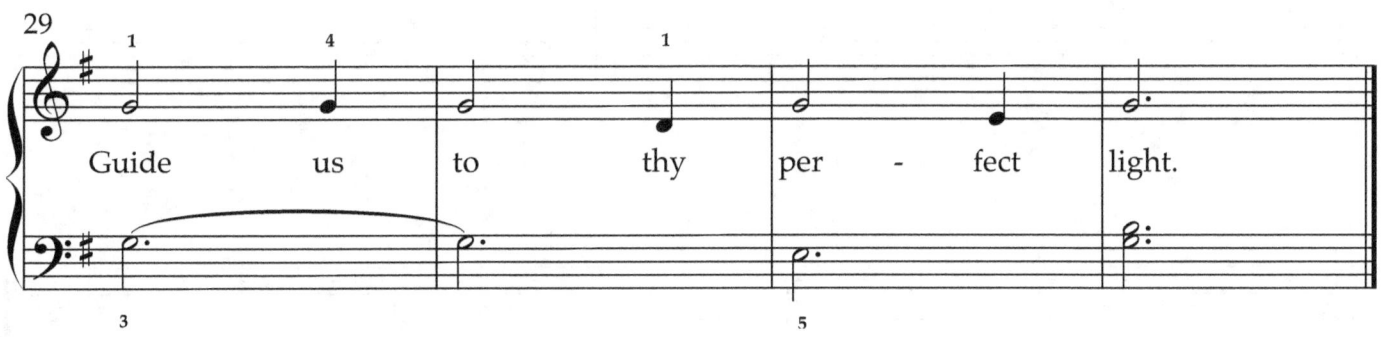

Jolly Old Saint Nicholas

Traditional

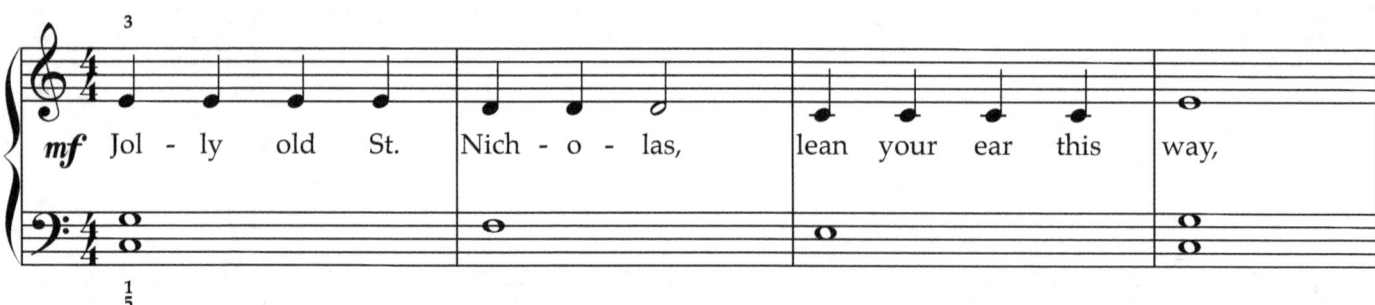

The First Noel

Traditional

Moderately slow

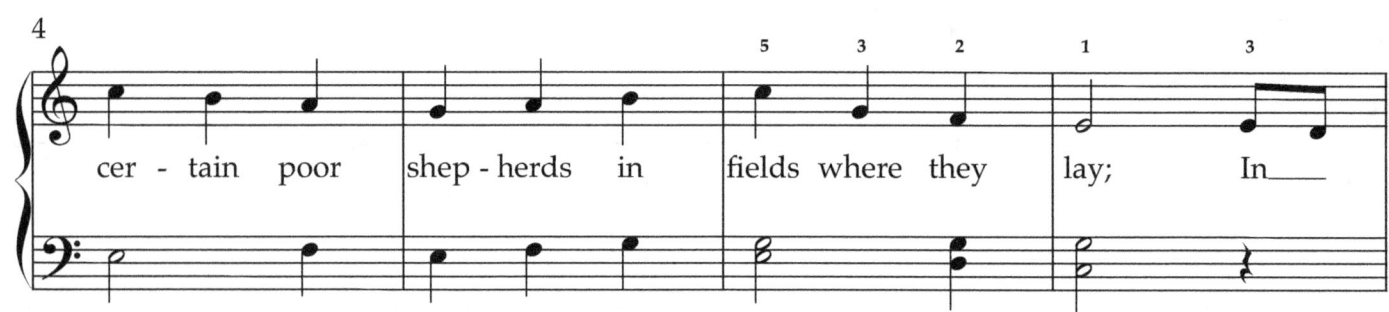

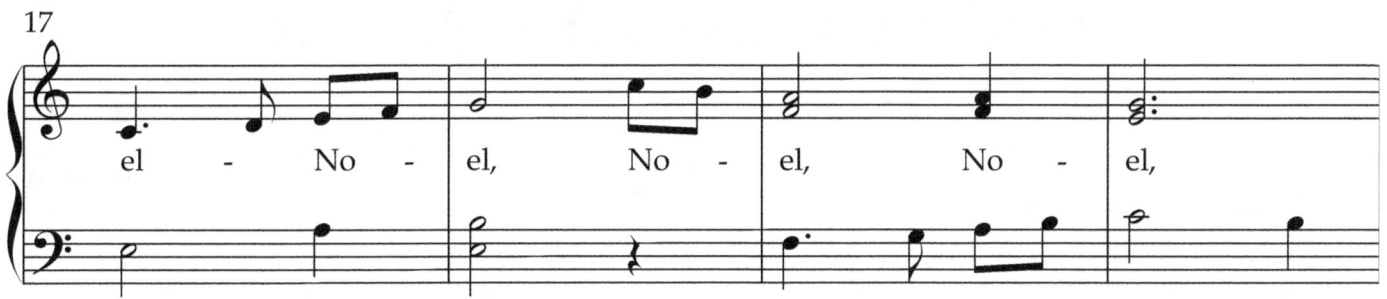
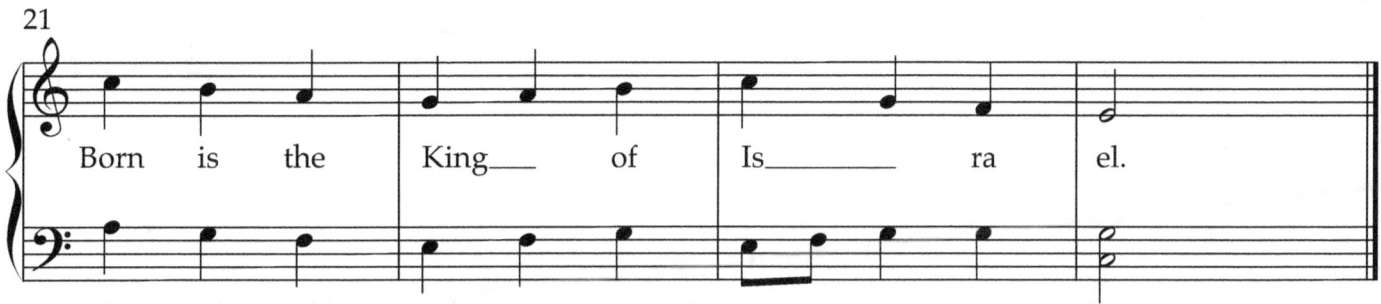

I Saw Three Ships

Traditional

The Coventry Carol

Traditional

Slowly

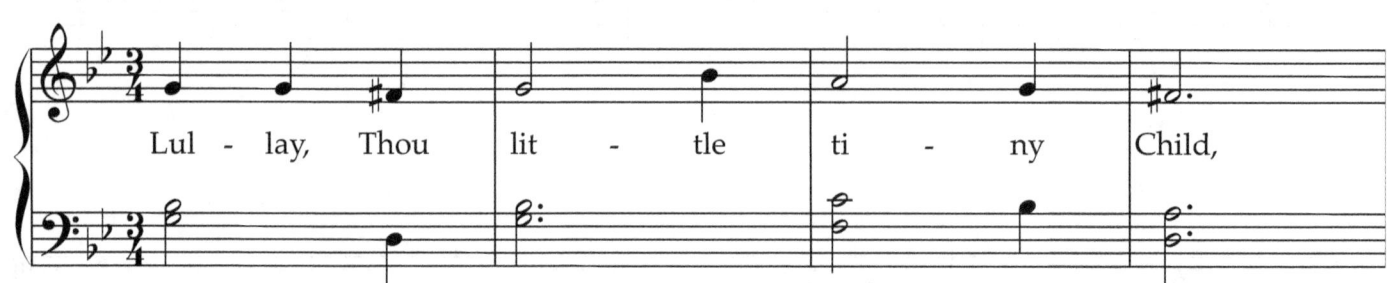

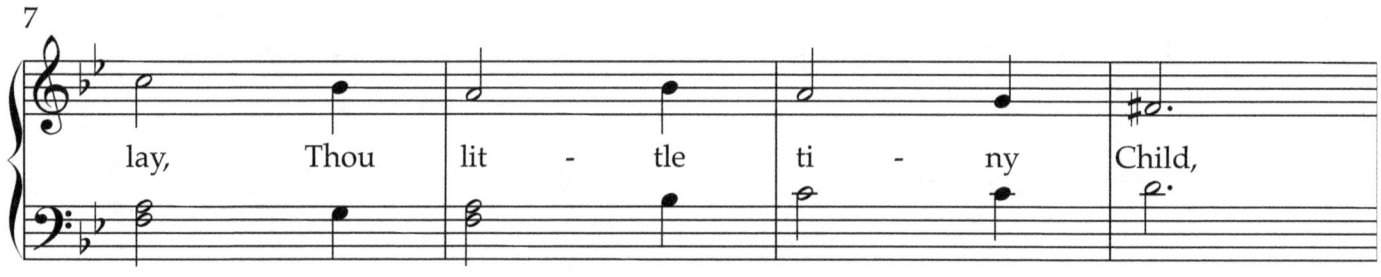

Good King Wenceslas

Traditional

Moderately

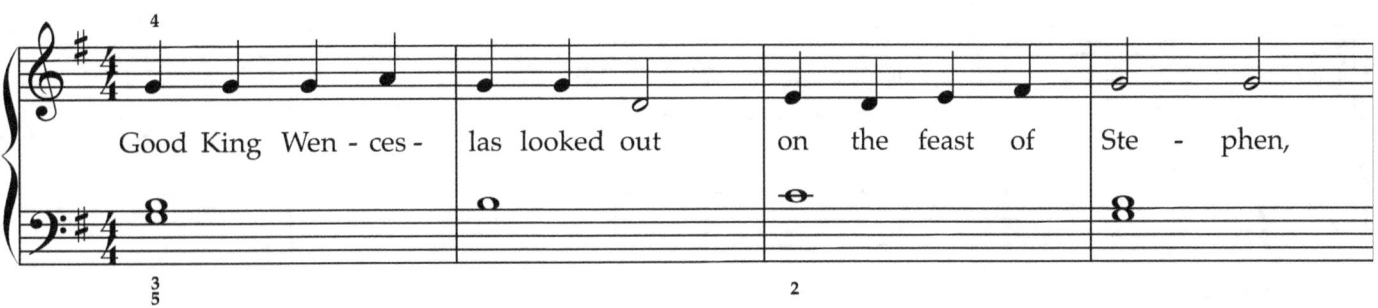
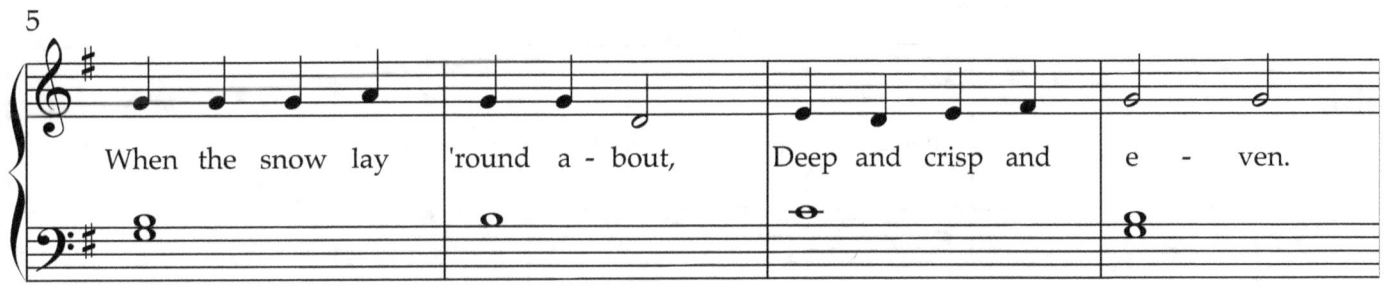
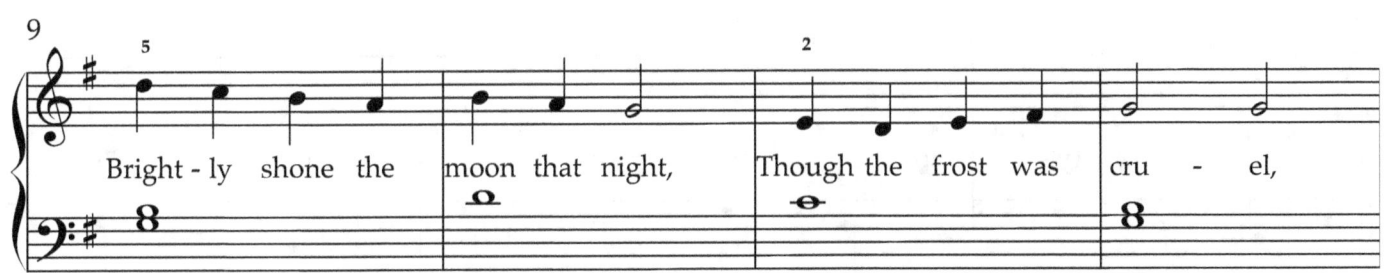
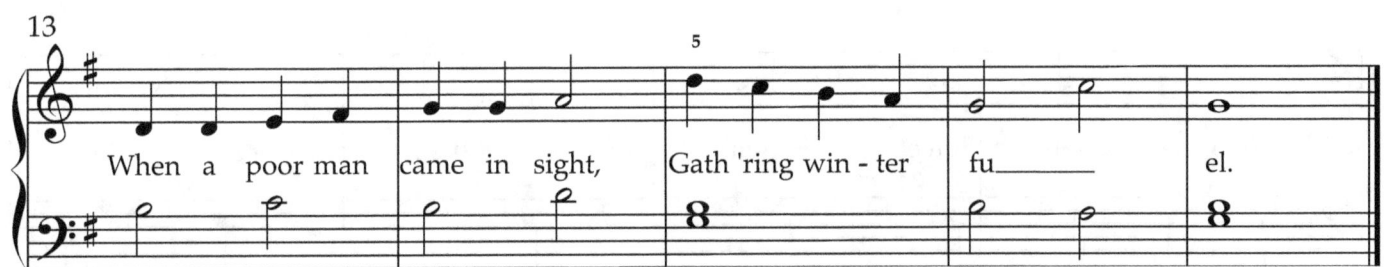

What Child is This?

English Traditional

Expressively

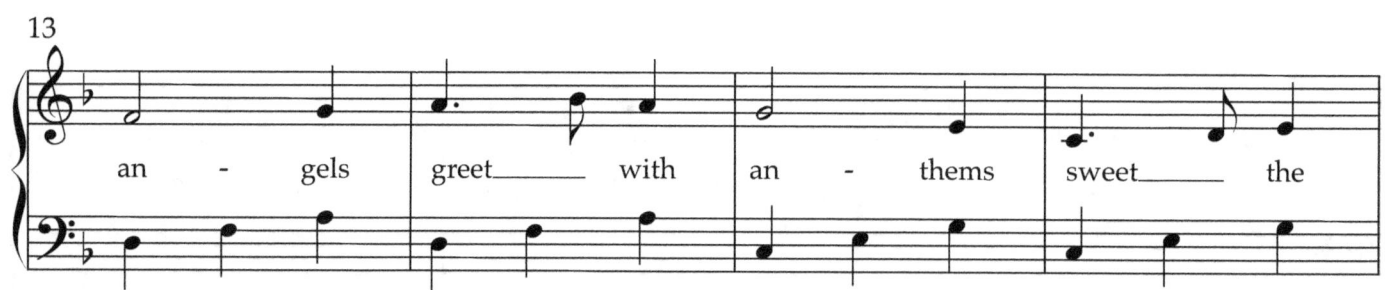

Auld Lang Syne

Scottish Traditional

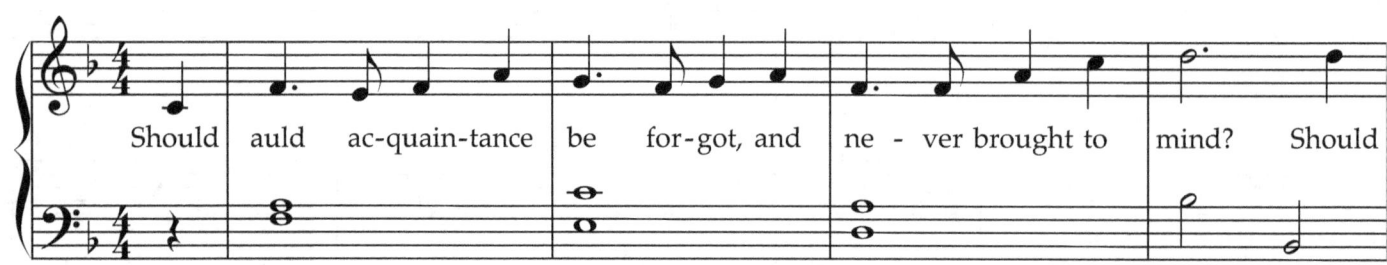

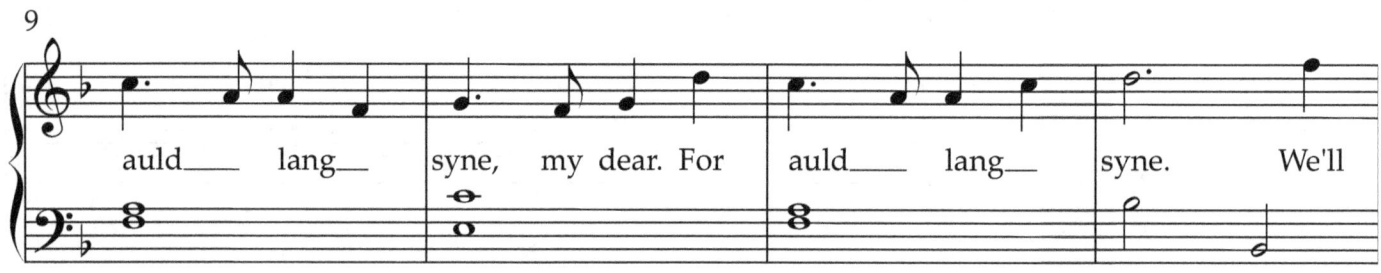
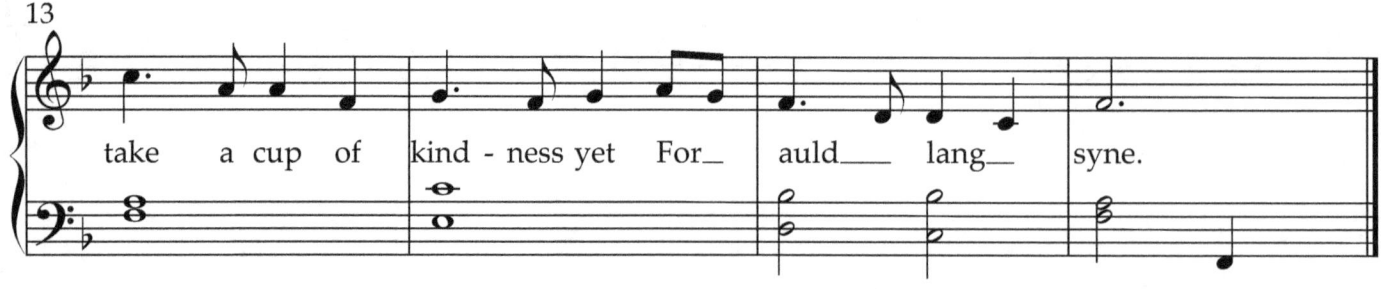